ISBN: 978-1-964411-09-5 (paperback)

Front cover image and book design by Amber Leigh Luecke

Printed in the United States of America

First printing edition 2024

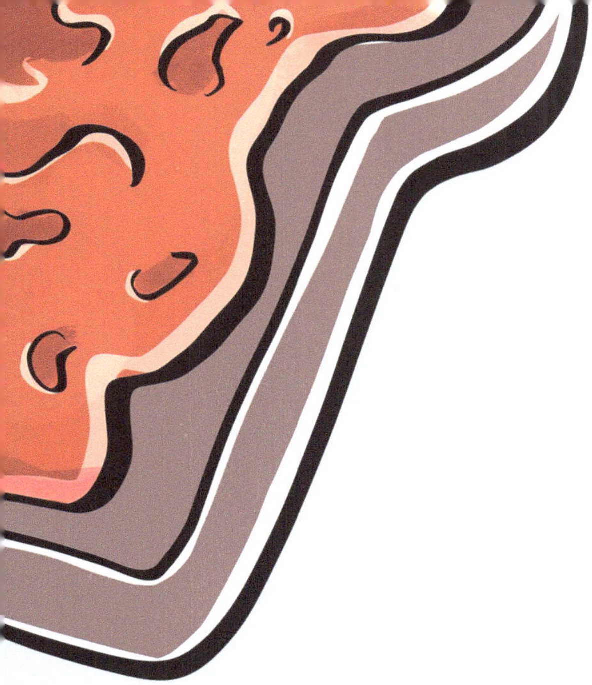

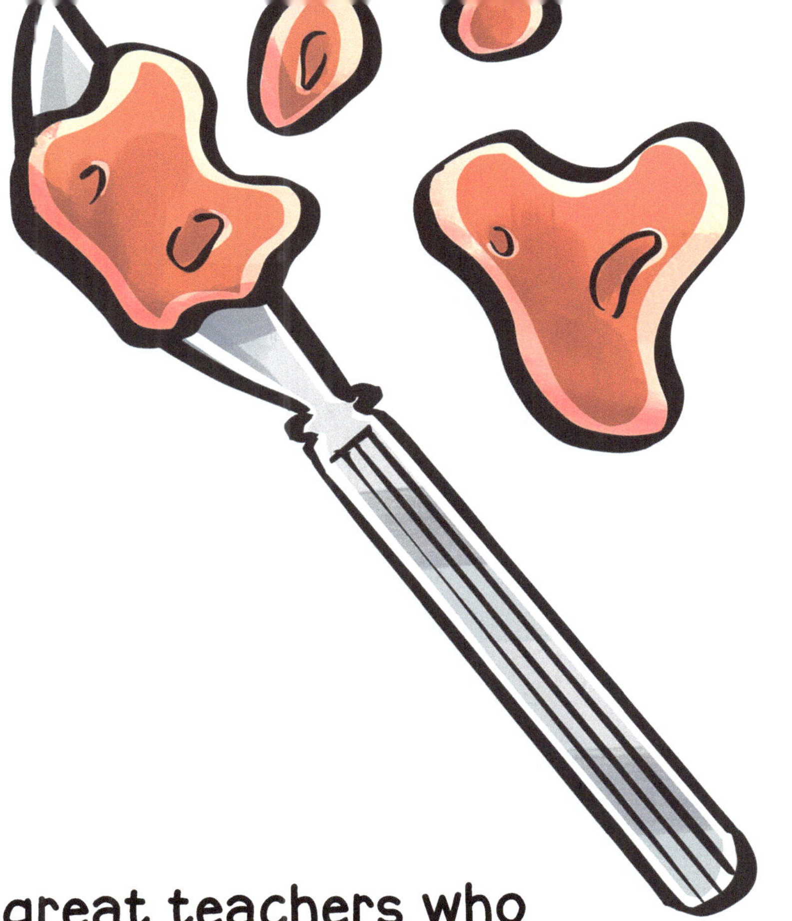

Dedicated to all of the great teachers who believe in their students.

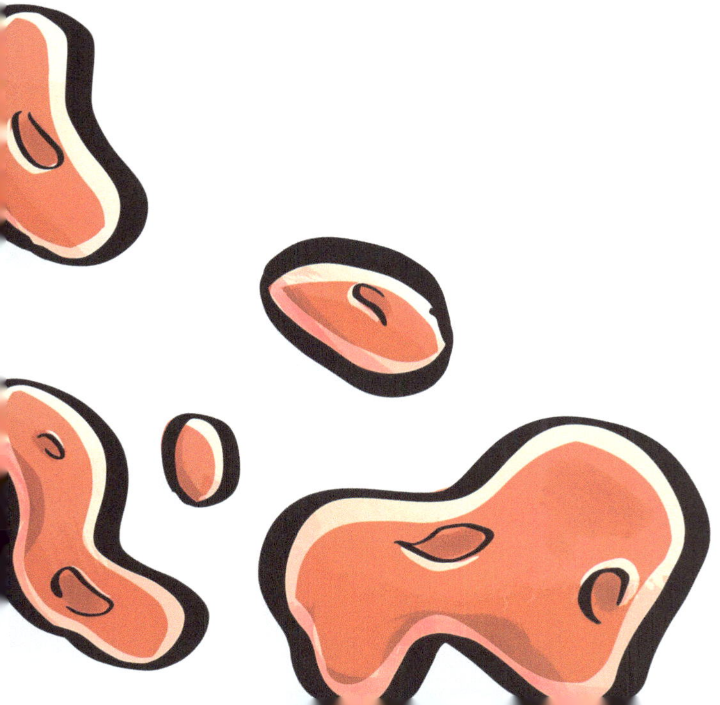

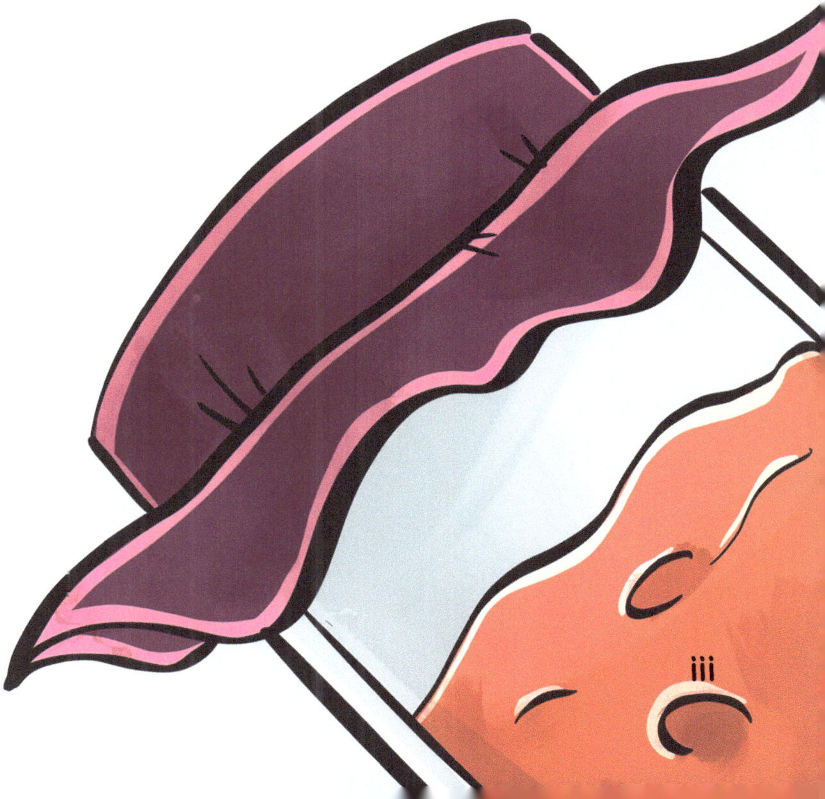

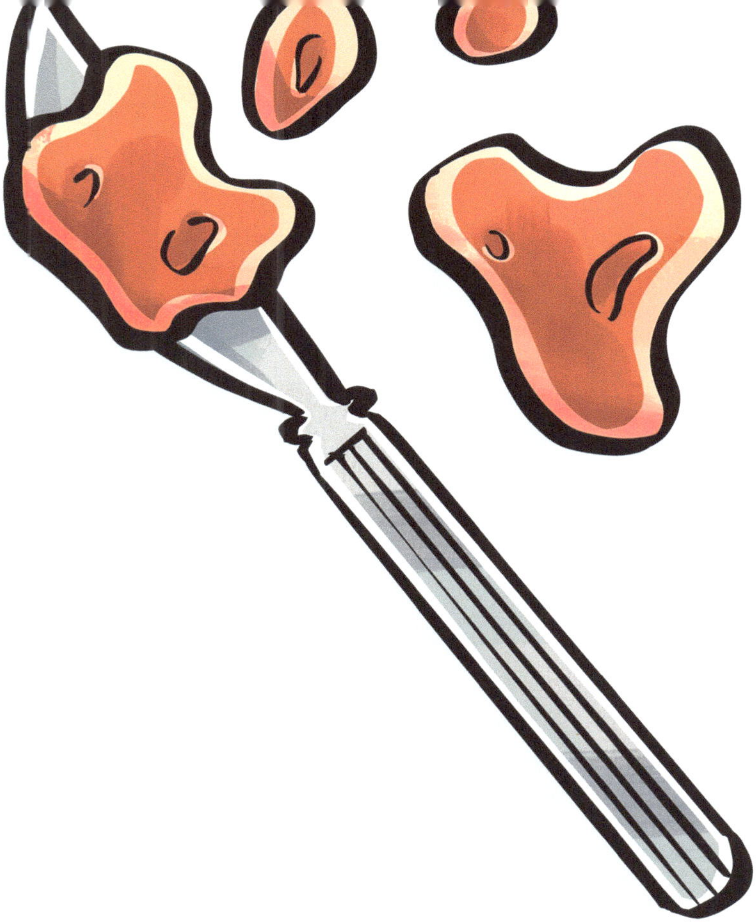

Jackie jumps for joy when her mom tells her they are making something special.

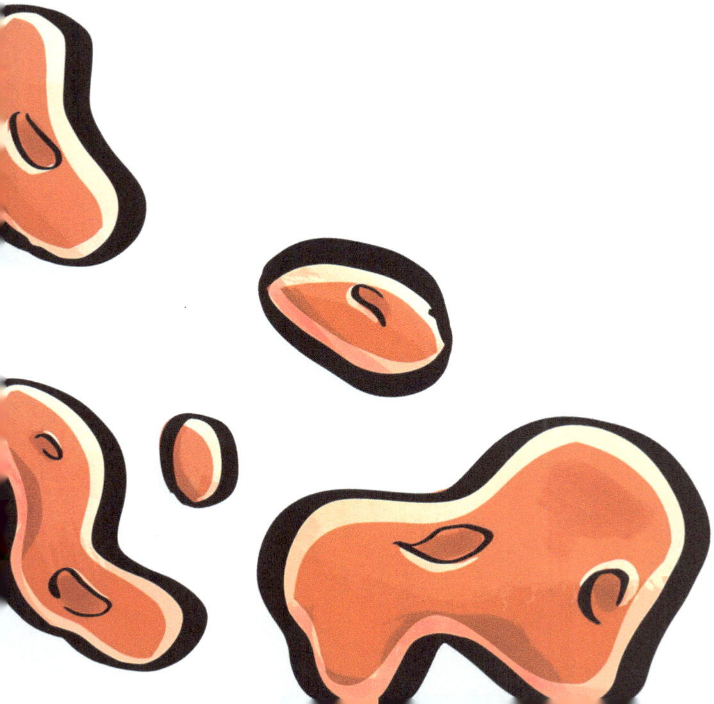

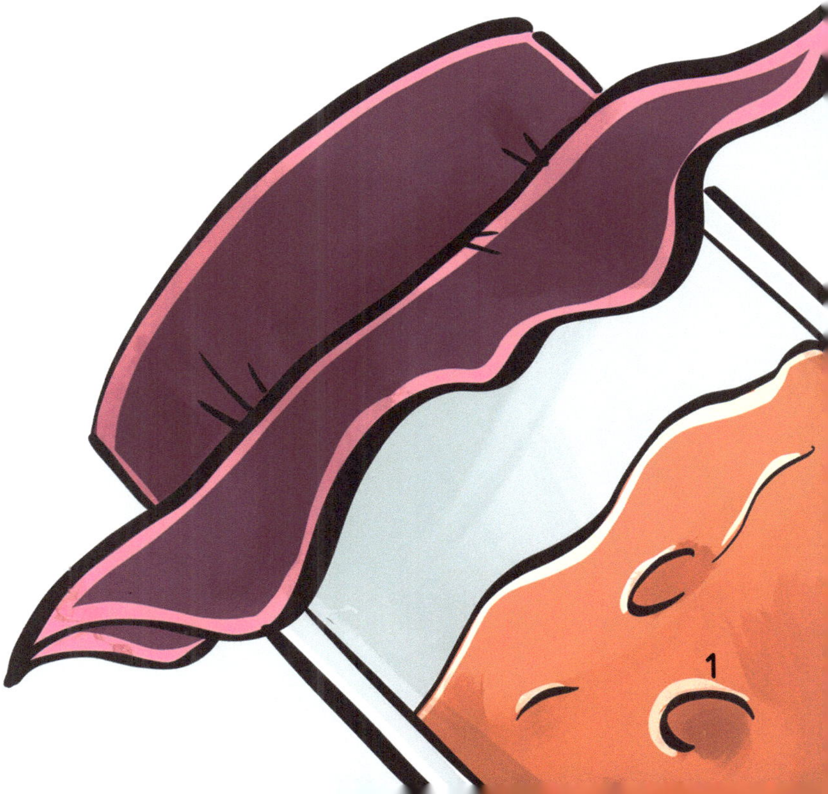

Her mom asks, "Can you guess the juicy job we're doing?"
Jackie thinks. Hmmm, what could she possibly have planned? Her mom says, "We are making Japanese jam!"

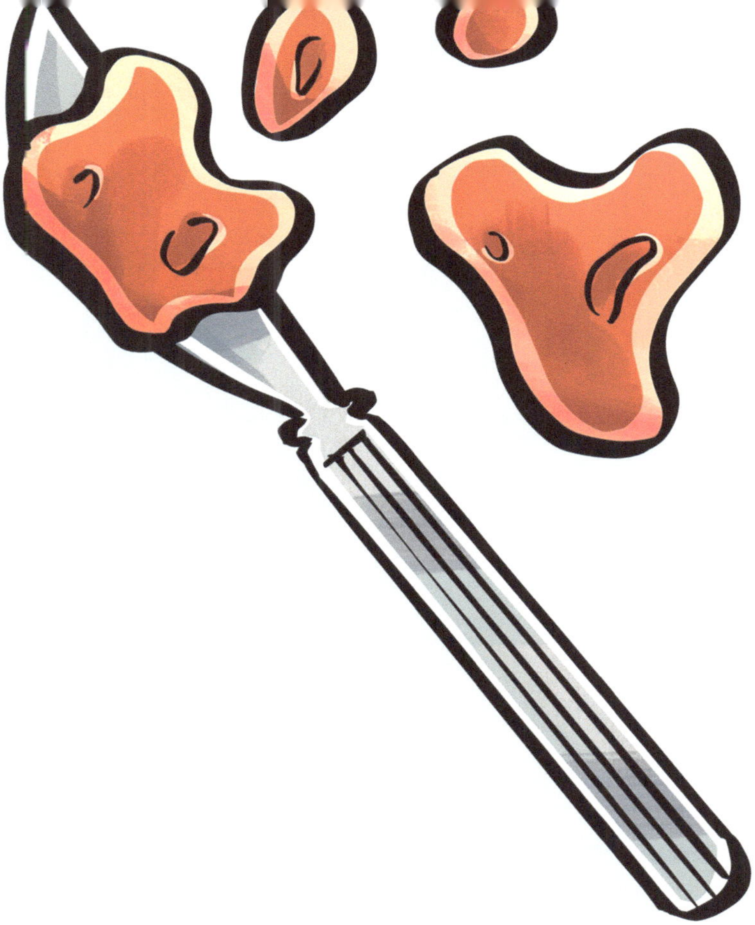

She gives Jackie a jar. Jackie is curious. She has never heard of Japanese jam.

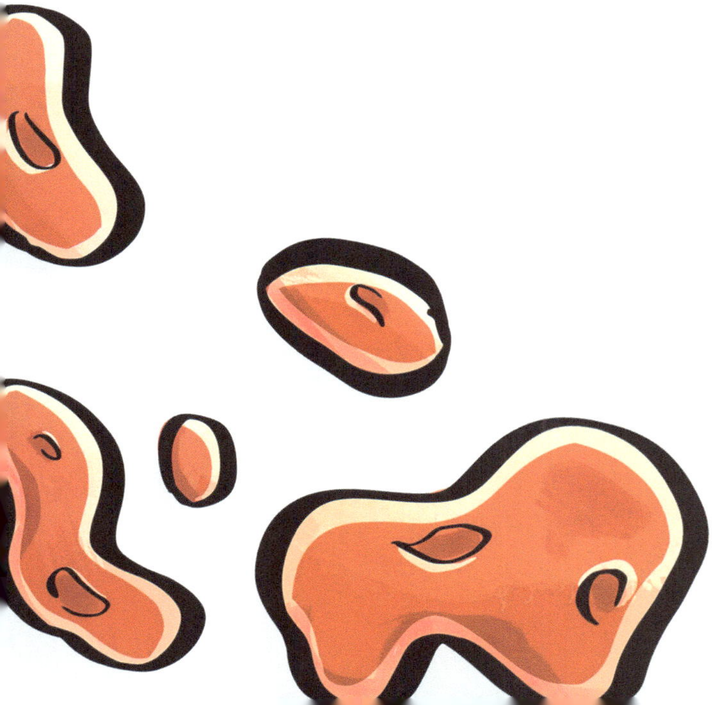

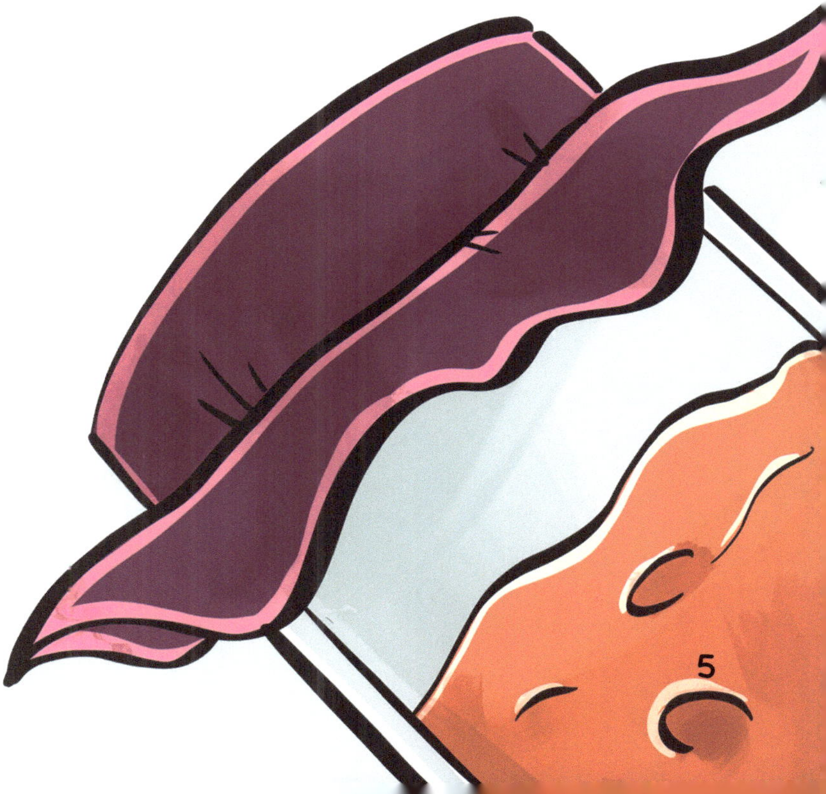

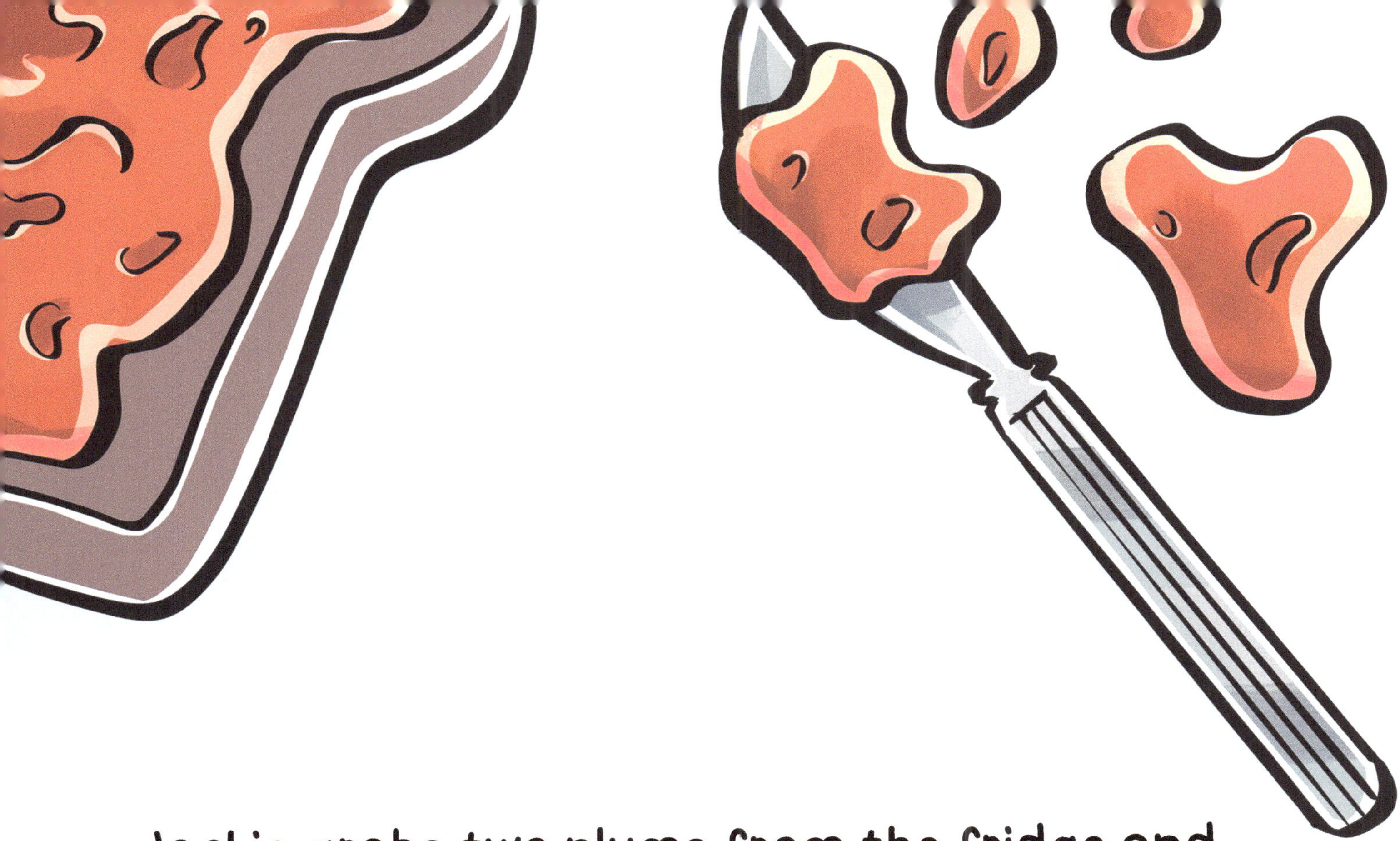

Jackie grabs two plums from the fridge and pits them. She smashes them into the jam jar and adds in the other ingredients.

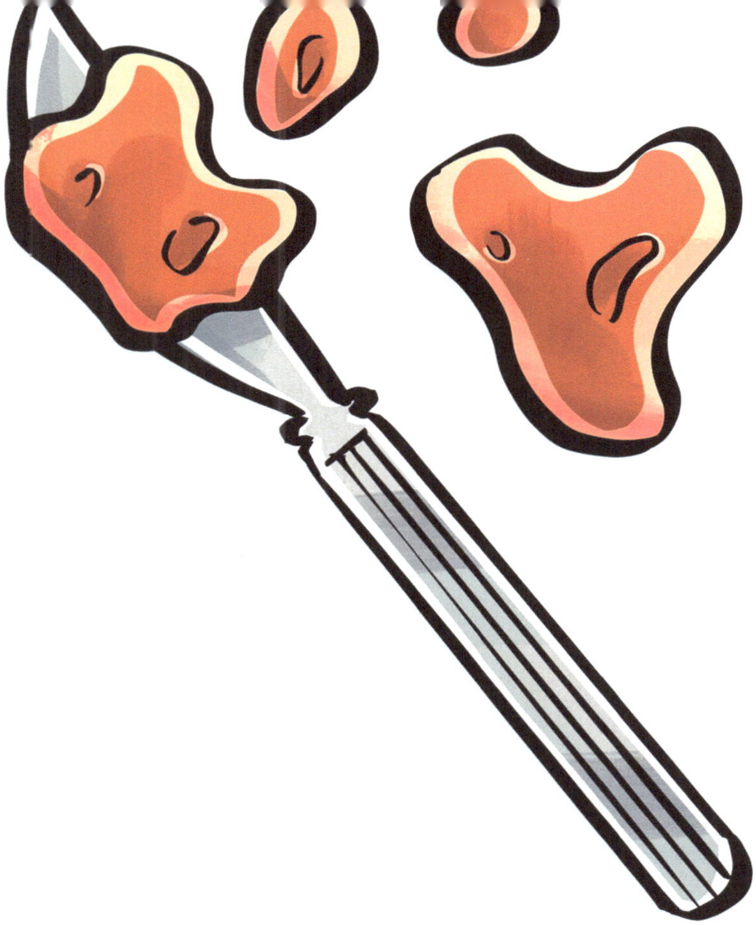

While the jam cools in the fridge, she jogs around the house in excitement.

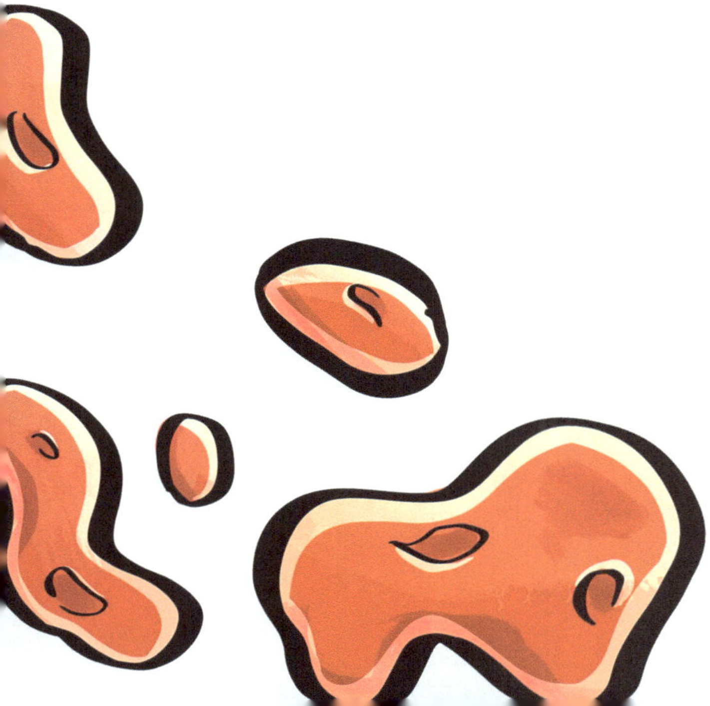

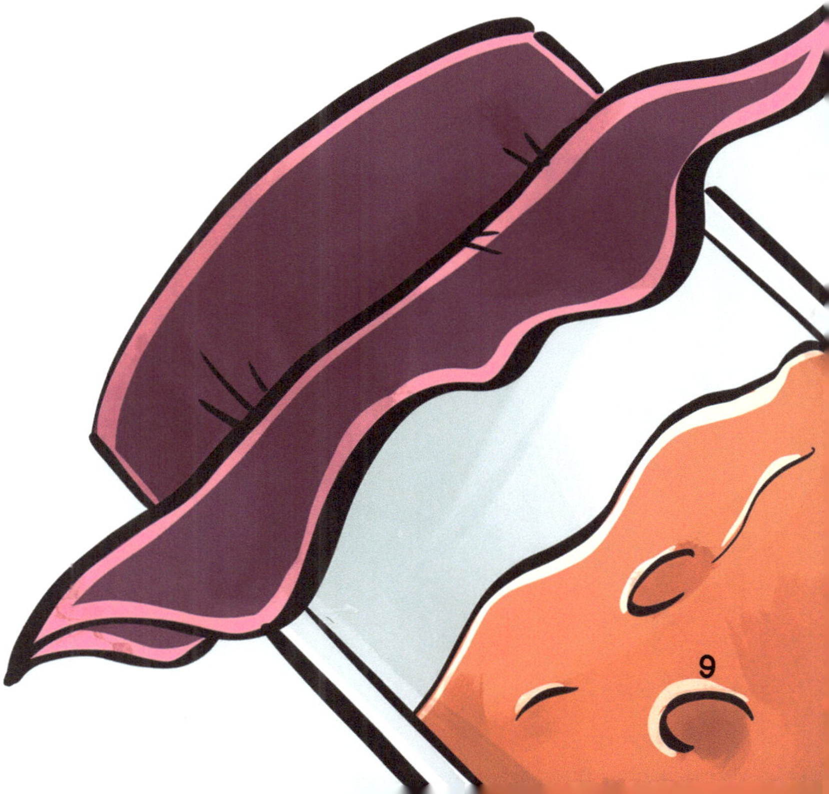

The jam cools, and Jackie makes toast.
She slops the jam on top of it. Jackie's mom
joins her in eating some. Jackie jumps high in the
air when she tastes the jam.

She runs aroud the house,
"Mmm! This is so good, Mom!"

Jackie's mom laughs,
"I should call you Jumpy Jackie."

"We hit the jam jackpot!" Jackie exclaims.

Jilly and Jane, Jackie's neighbors, see Jackie jumping around. They are curious to know why. Jane asks through the window, "Why are you jittering about, Jackie?"

13

Jackie hands Jane the jar of Japanese jam and watches Jane's jaw drop. "Isn't it delicious?" asks Jackie.

"It sure is!" says Jane. "It makes me want to jump and dance to jazz!"

Jilly tried some, and she jolts, jumps, and jogs around too. "Mmm!" she says. Everyone is enjoying the jam in the jar.

"Mom, what is the difference between jam and jelly?" Jackie asks with jam on her face.

Her mom laughs again. "Jelly comes from jellyfish, Jackie!"

"I'm going to write that in my journal!" says Jackie.

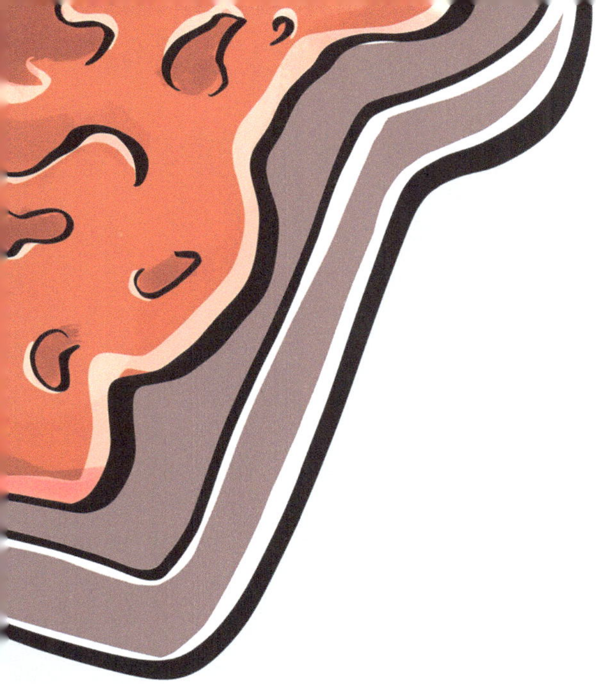

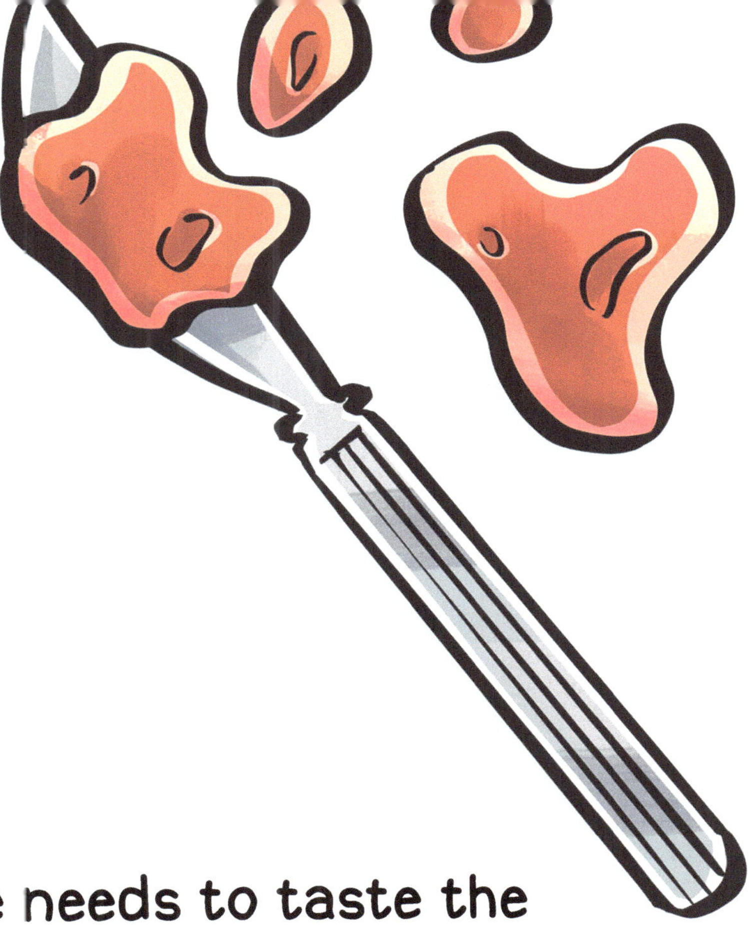

Jackie decides everyone needs to taste the Japanese jam. She hops in the Jeep with her mom and drives over to see her friends, Jack, John and Jade.

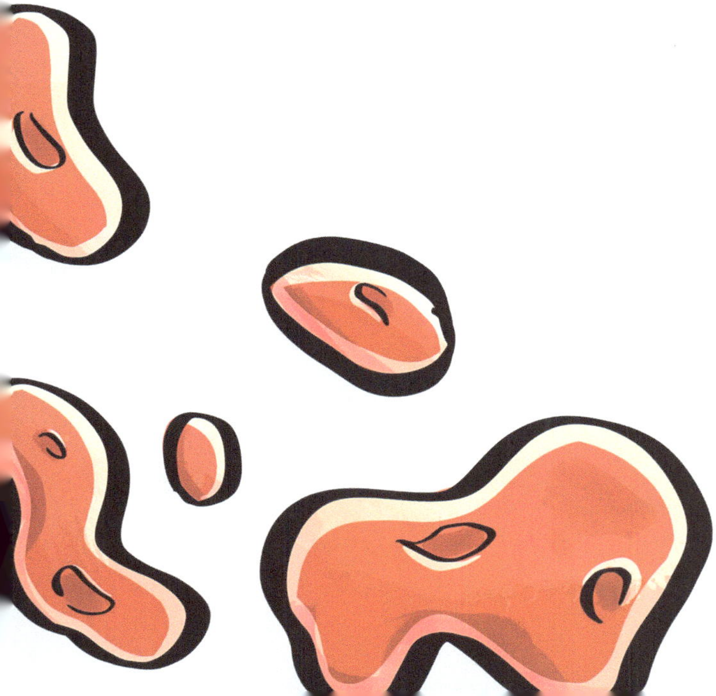

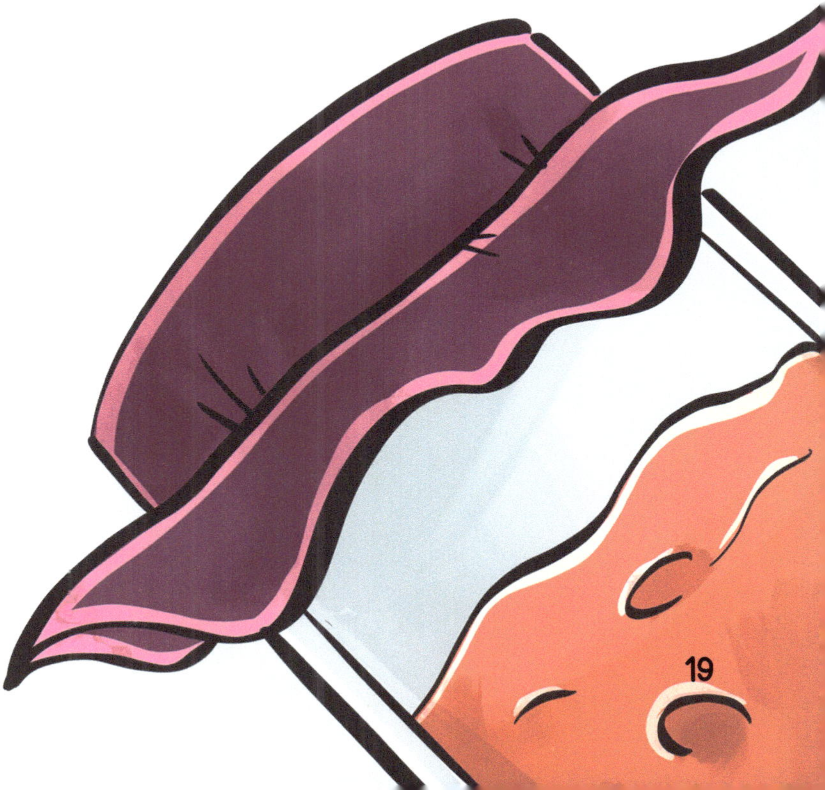

Jack, John, and Jade love the jam and want a jar for themselves.

"I'll be back in a jiffy!" Jackie says. She jogs back to the Jeep and comes back with more jars.

"Thanks, Jackie!" You did a great job with this jam!" Jade says as she puts the jam in her bag.

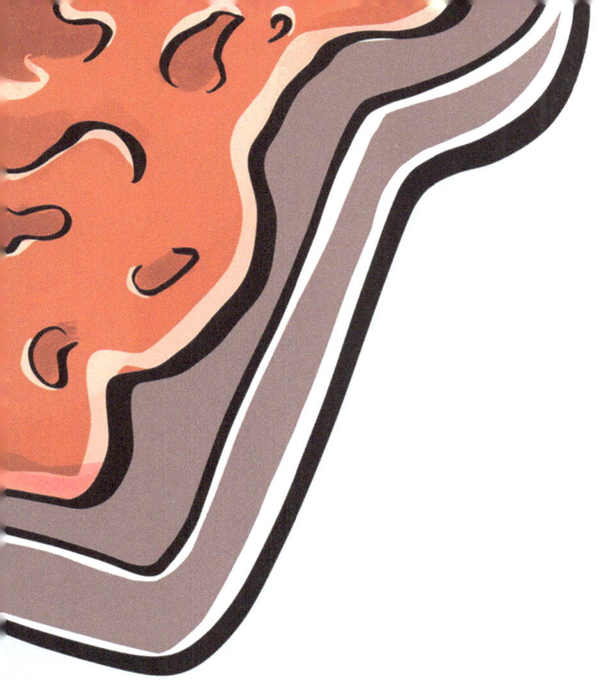

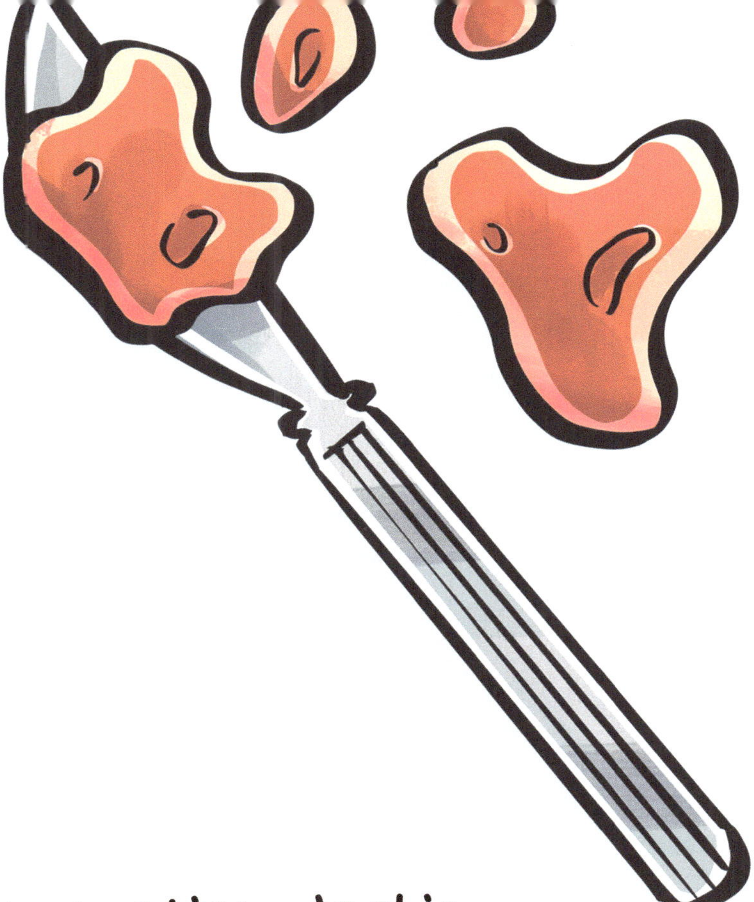

Jackie is proud of her creation. Jackie jumps for joy. She can't wait to make more Japanese jam soon!

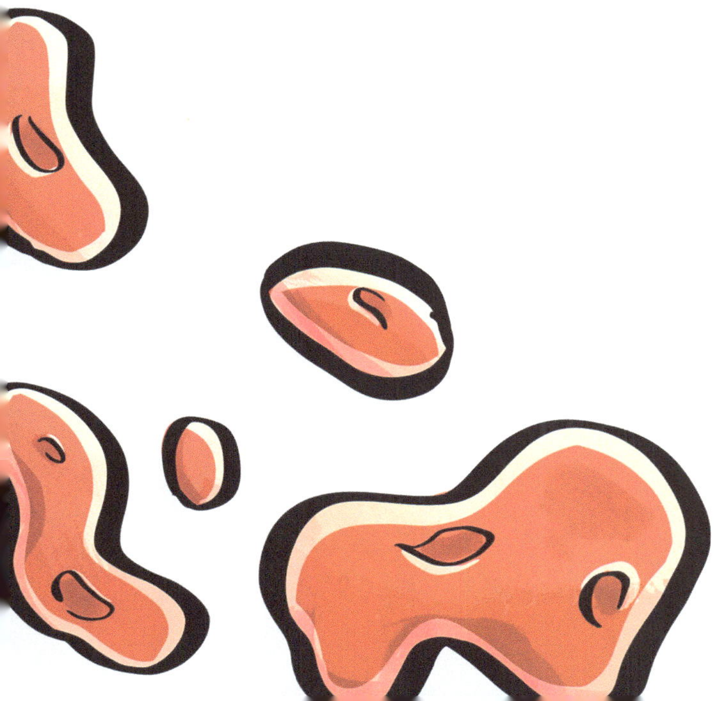

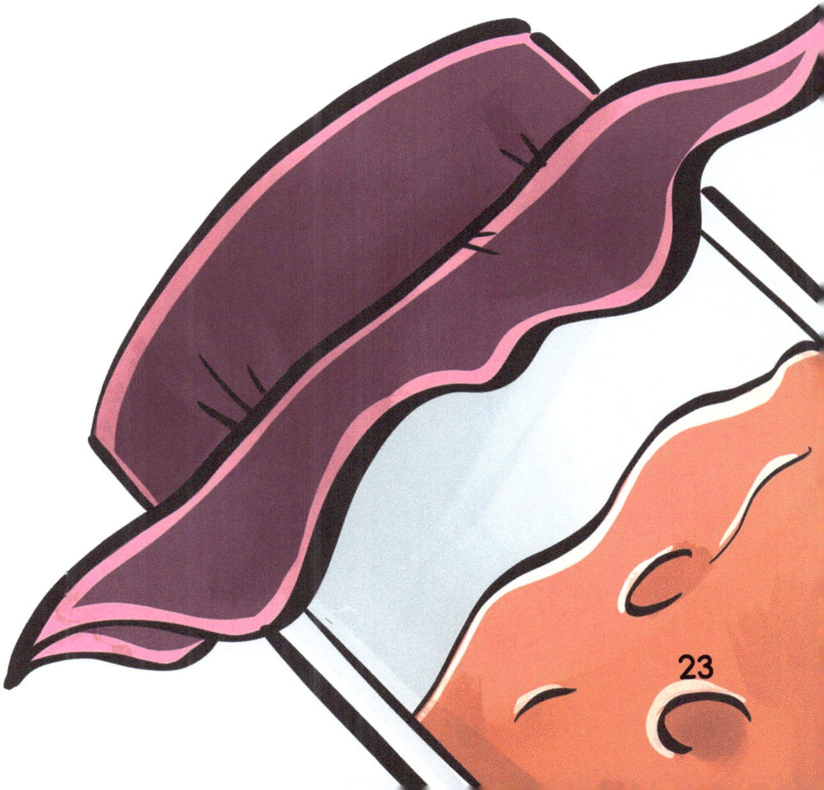

Discover the Wonders of Alliteration:
A Complete Collection from A to Z!

Dive into a world of wonder and learning with the "Alliteration Fun for All Types" Complete Collection, where each amusing story is dedicated to a specific letter of the alphabet.

From adventurous ants to zany zebras, these captivating tales are designed to engage and empower readers of all types, including those with dyslexia or other learning differences.

This collection of fun stories weaves rhythm, rhyming, and the magic of alliteration to foster a love of reading and promote inclusivity in storytelling.

Whether you're seeking an educational adventure, or inspiring a new reader, this collection promises to captivate young minds and instill a lifelong love for the magic of words.

To learn more visit Nickysbooks.com

If you enjoyed this book, please leave a review on Amazon and help new readers discover Nicky's books. Thank you.

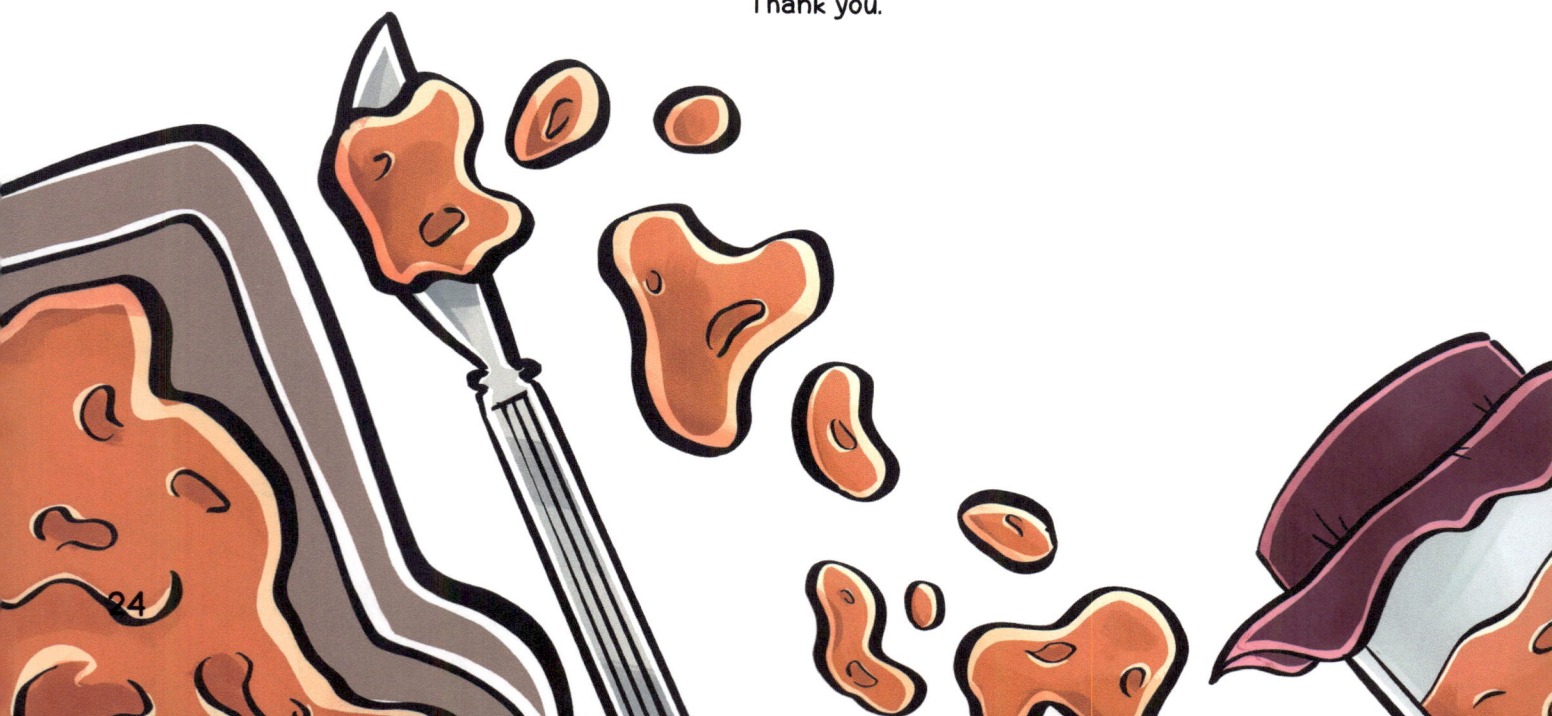